Everyday Dad

By:

Aaron Robert Jeffers

"Things may come to those who wait, but only the things left by those who hustle"

Abraham Lincoln

Landis, Gannon and Nyah! I love you and am honored to be your father and these words are for you!

My Dad knew my Mom would be there, so why did he think he did not need to be?

- Opportunity
- Denny's
- The First Thirteen
- Family
- Mickey
- Always There
- Robert Landis
- Lovie Love
- Who Gives Who
- Top Ten
- Super Dad vs. Everyday Dad
- Someday is Here
- A Lot's in a Name
- Forgive But Remember
- Future>Past
- I will …
- Game On

Forward

It is an unassuming Sunday afternoon in the summer and I am shooting basket after basket in our backyard.

It is the first day of school and I am starting middle school and just about everyone is new to me.

It is a Friday night and the Sonics are playing and I love watching basketball.

It is a weeknight and I have a lot of homework to do with a lot of questions.

It is a park with two gloves and a baseball, with a dad and his son having a catch.

It is when something great happens but also more so when it has been a tough day.

It is a Birthday, Christmas, Thanksgiving or Halloween.

It is the times I needed my dad the most, what can I say Mom other than thank you.

That's just the way it is! (or was) (but will not be for them)

Prologue

When I finally decided to put this together and get the words down on paper I knew I was ready. I felt ready because I would not be coming from an angry place. I wanted to write about the things that happened with my Dad and how they impacted me through the years. I felt organized in my thoughts. I wrote the words, but I feel the experiences told the story. Everything in these chapters happened and is true from my memory. I would feel honored for people to read this and not feel alone. If you are a child without your dad or did not have him growing up I hope this finds you. I hope my words will support and inspire you to be active in a child's life. I decided a long time ago to do my best and father a different path than I had growing up. I feel it is a work in progress and I learn every day to be the dad that I want to be. I love being a parent and I really don't feel there is anything that is more important. Do you? My heart, that is what Landis, Gannon and Nyah will get. Twenty-four / seven / twelve / fifty-two / three-sixty-five, (with of course a few exceptions). Parents, you know what I'm talking about!

Opportunity

The year is 2009 and it is Christmas night. This was the 8th Christmas that my wife and I had spent together, but it would not be like any other before it. Christmas is a great time of year and it just happens that our first son Landis was trying to come as a late present. As we drove from our house in North Seattle to the birthing center in Downtown Seattle I was nervous, very nervous. Gina was already in labor and all of this was new to us. It seemed like things were all moving so fast. Our own child would be here soon!

We get to the hospital and get checked in and a part of me still cannot believe this is happening. I really hope that I am ready for this. I will keep telling myself that. As I help my wife get out of the car and get up to the correct floor everything seems like a blur. Wait, how did we get here? It was a very long night into the next day but it was an experience that I know I will never forget. I was there from the beginning and this is already something that I am proud of.

It did turn out that Landis did not want to be born on Christmas. He was born the next day on the 26th in the afternoon. I still remember the room that we were in and how many of our friends and family came. And no, my dad was not one of those people who was there.

When I held my son for the first time I was filled with so many emotions. He was so little! I had been a preschool teacher and had a fairly good understanding of what was to come, but if I was being truthful I really didn't. Having a child, if you do it right will change your life forever. I definitely always wanted children. As I hold Landis I wonder what is in store for us. I know one thing for sure, I will be there for him and in his life. I have no doubt about that. I would not be able to live with myself if I was not. I think deep down past all of the emotions that I am feeling and I know this is an opportunity. An opportunity to do something great! An opportunity to be a father to my son! MY SON! I am hopeful. I am excited. I am terrified. I am feeling so much love. I am determined. I am exhausted. We were up all night. Of course I am nowhere near as tired as my wife. Today I am a father. Tomorrow I am a father. Day one of this path that we have started with our son! Where does this path lead? Well, I am not sure but I will be there. I am prepared with a really big backpack and lot of supplies. I have internalized a lot of what happened to me growing up and these are what I hope will be my most useful tools. My Dad, unfortunately his backpack was pretty small. He was not prepared for the long journey.

Denny's

It is a cold day in January of 2004 and my brother and I are driving through the Ballard neighborhood of Seattle to Denny's, a chain restaurant. As the streets pass by I am thinking what this breakfast will be like. This is a breakfast I have looked forward to and not looked forward to for the last thirteen years. How do I approach my Dad who I have not seen since I was thirteen years old?

There have been no letters, phone calls or emails and it is too early for text messages. I have so many questions, but I am not sure I even want the answers. As we pull up to the parking lot and find a spot at Denny's, my heart starts racing and I dig deep to control all the emotions that are running through me. I still deep down wonder if he will show up. This is something that I always wanted, to clear the air, to get everything out there. To talk about why and how all of this happened.

I get out of the car and for the first time in a very long time since I was a very young man I will see my Dad (I think) in person and ask the question I have wanted to ask as long as I can remember, why? I know there is probably not an answer that will ever satisfy me, but I need to ask this before moving forward in any kind of way with him. Does he even deserve that? I don't know? As the door's open to the restaurant and I actually see my Dad I am struck with fear that maybe I am not ready for this, but I keep walking towards him. I am proud of myself for doing this and then it hits me. Will we shake hands, hug or something else? What do I want, I don't know? I am now feet away from him and a million thoughts are in my head, including will he pay for breakfast? He better, as it has been a really long time coming.

This little gathering is happening because my older brother is getting married in a few months and decided to invite our dad to the wedding. My brother had decided about six months prior to that to start building a relationship with our dad. I was not as ready for that as he was. I am happy for my brother but having our dad there is a little hard for me. To be honest it is extremely hard. I support my brother and don't want the first time that I see my Dad in a very long time to be at my brother's wedding, so here we are. My brother has set this up and I believe my Dad knows why. I hope this goes well or there might be a bit of a problem with the wedding in a couple of months. Oh, and did I mention it is a small wedding and I am the best man. I guess what it really comes down to is just having breakfast with my brother and Dad, right? People do that all the time! That is not something that I am familiar with.

I had been to this Denny's many times before growing up in Ballard, but I had no idea that this restaurant would represent such a huge crossroads in the relationship and struggle with my Dad. Ironically as I write this the Denny's is not even standing anymore, but I still remember the booth we sat in. I remember where I sat, where my Dad sat and brother as well.

My brother is next to me and I make eye contact with my Dad and shake his hand. We wait a few minutes and then they seat us. We make small talk and he asks how I am doing. I say something but I am not really sure how to answer. If he really cared how I was doing why didn't he ask a lot earlier than today? I can sense that he missed me, but that just gives me more questions. I guess you could say I missed him to. He is still my Dad. We order our food and then my Dad asks me the question I have thought about for a very long time. I have always wondered if I was asked how I would answer. Would I get angry, sad, poetic or something else? I am a little shocked that finally what I have always wanted is here right in front of me. My Dad has asked, "So your brother said there were some things you wanted to talk about". It just flies through my head as I hear the words, "Yeah you could say that, I have just a few things to discuss". I say these words only in my head. I know I should not be surprised but I still am by his tone, that he is a little uncertain as to why I have questions. I guess there are always things in life that just are a little hard to understand.

I knew this breakfast was happening so I believe I am prepared to say what I want. Wait, am I. $#!*, I guess I don't have a choice now. Honestly I don't remember what I actually said first, but I do remember what I really wanted to ask. My brother is mostly quiet during this time and I understand why because these are my questions not his. The words and feelings are mine not his. I ask my Dad why? Why weren't you there all of this time? He missed so much time. Why did you miss so many basketball games that I played in? Why did you miss every single graduation? Why so many birthdays lost? No cards sent, nothing. Basically where the #@^% were you? I know there is no response that will be enough, but it feels like forever waiting for what he will say. His response was kind and calm, half strange half satisfying. He somehow made me feel more confused, yet I feel much clearer about things. He says that he did not think that we wanted him around. WAIT, WHAT? You're our dad you should have fought to be there! I realize what I think I always knew, my Dad truly does not and did not understand the impact of him not being in our lives has had. Very hard to swallow that one! He does apologize for not doing more and this gives me something. I am left feeling somewhat satisfied, but still confused. I don't know if we will ever talk about this again or even if I want to. Really there is nothing for him to say other than that he really screwed up.

We finish our food and start to walk out together. We talk in the parking lot more and it occurs to me that I know I will see him again soon for the first time in a really long time. As we talk I have thoughts about the future and where things go from here. What am I ready for? What is he capable of? We say our goodbyes and drive away. Will things be different, the same or better? What path will this lead to? I don't know?

I am not married but have a girlfriend that I live with. We have been dating for three years and I love her. I wonder driving away will I be a good father? Will we get married? Will we have boys or girls? I don't know? One thing I do know if all of those things happen I will be there for our children. I have learned that lesson all too hard.

The First Thirteen

My parents divorced when I was three years old. I have no memory of them being together or my dad living in the home that we grew up in. My brother was six when they divorced and he has some memories of us all living together. Our parents were married pretty young, which is what people did in the late 1960's. My Mom's family grew up in San Francisco and she moved up to Seattle to be with my Dad, so if this did not happen I would not be living in Seattle. I love Seattle. I love my beautiful wife and our three children (Nyah's ETA September 2017). We have great friends and family in the Pacific Northwest. I am a true Seattleite! I love the Seahawks, Mariners and Sonics ☹. I love Green Lake and Seattle Center. The Space Needle! I love that there are seasons and it really does not rain all the time. I am truly proud that I grew up here. I love the house we grew up in and that my Mom still lives in today. Who knows what life would be like if my Mom did not move to Seattle. I could be a 49ers fan (yuck). It is interesting to me that my Mom's decision to marry my Dad changed the course of basically the entire family and I am glad she did it.

For the first thirteen years I was on this earth my Dad was in and out of my life. I am truly not writing this to make anyone feel bad, but people make decisions and have to live with the outcome of those decisions. The first thirteen years were not like the next thirteen but just about all of it was hard with my Dad. My Dad re-married pretty quickly after the divorce and we would go and see him from time to time in their Edmonds home. Edmonds is about 20 minutes from Ballard, just an FYI. It was always uncomfortable for me though. I used to get stomach aches before he would come and not want to go. This did not help the situation at all. But when I did go we would drive down to Tacoma where his mother lived. His mom would make dinner and would make the same dinner every single time and I did not like her food. I tried to eat but I was just a kid. I may sound spoiled, but I think there were other things in play. So, because I did not really eat she gave me giant horse size vitamins. Super fun! She gave me the vitamins because she thought I was not getting enough nutrition from eating food. Whatever the reason I just could not get it together there. However, it was not bad all the time during these years. When we went down to visit my Dad's side of the family they were nice to us and I still got the feeling of family. I remember sitting in my grandmother's kitchen and playing games. I remember going down stairs and playing down there as well. The people were nice and under other circumstances I am sure I would have looked at things differently. I don't have a lot of memories for things we did during these years with my Dad. I feel bad about this because I know we did things. The remaining memories I have include, my brother and I would go over and stay with our dad and hang out with the son of his second wife. They had a nice house. I just have a really hard time remembering a lot of what we did.

I do have many memories of doing things with my Mom. I remember so many Mariners games, driving home from school listening to 106.9 on the radio, reading books every night before bed, pizza in the U-District after school, feeding the ducks in the arboretum, stopping for snacks before school at the gas station, church sweats, going to Friday Harbor to visit grandma and grandpa, going to the ocean, hot chocolate, Sonics games, the little red car, and her putting concrete in our backyard so I could play basketball. Before that I used to go back and shoot for hours on grass, boards and dirt. I remember one specific Mariners game, June 2, 1990 when Randy Johnson threw the first no-hitter in Mariners History and we were there, just her and I. I remember the one game playoff in 1995 that the Mariners won to go to the playoffs for the first time, again just her and I. Oh and you are probably wondering what church sweats are. I was a young man who enjoyed being comfortable so we compromised on what I would wear, so there were sweatpants that I only wore to church. Don't judge, the sweatpants were pretty nice!

I guess what it comes down to is my Mom worked her tail off with us. She got her Master's Degree with two crazy boys running around. My Dad took the easy way out and did not fulfill his responsibilities. I used to get so angry when I was young when I thought about my Dad. When a parent chooses not to be there it is a hard thing for a child to understand. Unfortunately all too many children know this feeling like I do. I will never have our kids carry that with them. They will know a father who is there and supportive and gives as much as I can give. This is what pushes me! I want more than anything to be there for our children and to provide for them what I did not have, a father not a sometimes dad. Every child deserves that. I don't believe I would feel as strongly about this if what happened had not happened. I struggle with that. Did my Dad actually help me to be a better father? Wrap your head around that one!

My mom taught me to always be there to support your children no matter what. She taught me that hard work pays off no matter what. She taught me to be kind and generous to others and treat people how you want to be treated. She is a person you can count on to do the things that are important in life, plain and simple. Is there really anything more important than that? Every child deserves to have as many people as possible to love them unconditionally in their life. This is what I want for our children and for every child. Our children are lucky to have a wonderful mother who works so hard to make sure they feel special. But of course I had that too.

One of the things that I remember growing up is playing basketball. I would have games once a week and my Dad would say at times that he would be coming. Well, let's just say it is hard for a child to understand why other dads were there and his was not. I loved playing basketball when I was growing up. I worked really hard at it and would spend hours playing. It was my passion and for my Dad not to support my passion was really very difficult. What was more important on a Saturday than being at my basketball game? I sure can't think of anything.

As time went on and we got closer to my brother starting college and likely moving away I had no idea what was coming, No one did. The summer before my brother's senior year we toured a number of colleges in Washington State. I was sad he might be moving away but I was happy for him that he was going to start a new journey. The craziness that was to come, well that was almost unthinkable.

My Dad was a contributing member of society. He was a firefighter. You were not expecting that, I'll bet. I do remember going to his fire station, which was about three miles from our house. Crazy right! He literally drove by our house to get to work. That is just ridiculous. I can joke about it now, but that was very hard for me growing up. Anyway, my Dad was a firefighter. Cool, right? Well, I don't remember telling people when I was growing up. Wonder why?

As time got closer to my brother finishing high school, things become harder and harder with my Dad. I truly still do not know everything that happened but basically he tried to get my brother to join the military and not go to college. I know this was hard on all of us but mostly on my brother. I am sad he had to go through that. This changed everything and this is what caused the empty thirteen years. Honestly, I am not really sure what he thought was going to happen? My brother resisted the military and wanted to go to school. It got really messy and had to be dealt with legally. Not fun to try and get your own dad to help pay for your college. My brother made the right choice he is a very successful businessman now and works in the technology field. My Dad however made a decision based on money and it cost him a lot more than that. I like to think and hope that if Dad could go back and change that decision he would, maybe he would, maybe he wouldn't, hey maybe I will ask him, maybe not.

The last conversation I had with my Dad when I was thirteen was on the phone. I did not know at the time that it would be such a long time until I would talk with him again. I had to tell him that I was not comfortable going to a Seahawks game with him. I love the Hawks! Doing this was very hard and I felt it was very unfair to be put in that position by him.

About five years later it was the fall of 1996 and my basketball season was starting it was my senior year of high school. I had worked very hard the first three years of high school so I could start and play one year of varsity basketball at one of the quality schools in the City of Seattle (Ballard High School). I remember my Mom asking me, "Do you want to ask your dad to come to any games?" I remember feeling so torn. I want him to come, but I want him to really want to be there.

However, I cannot handle being disappointed again. I remember thinking what's the word: #^@%! My Dad did not come to any of the games. I just was not ready for all of that yet. His loss I guess. Whatever our kids are doing in high school I will be there to support them. They will not know that feeling.

My Dad has made some major mistakes in his life that made things harder for people, people that should have been able to count on him. He has to my knowledge never committed a crime (that I know of ☺). I do believe not being there for your children, in my humble opinion, is worthy of a crime. He does support his younger brother who has a mental disability and has for a long time. He is flawed but don't we all make mistakes? A lot of freedom can come from letting go of what other people have done to you! I try and remember this every time I see my Dad.

Family

My Dad had his dad in his life growing up and my Mom tells me he was a positive role model for him. I have no memory of my Dad's dad. My Mom had her father in her life as well and he was in my life until I was seventeen years old. When he passed away it was hard for our entire family and things did change. My oldest son carries his middle name as his first name "Landis". My second son carries his first name as his middle name "Robert". I still miss him and wish I could have introduced him to my wife and our three children. I have one tattoo and it reads our son's two names as well as my grandpa. I will soon have a second tattoo that will be our daughter's name. No one names their children after people they don't love or respect. We should all strive to be this positive influence.

I am the only current father in my immediate biological family. My brother does not have children or my uncle. From the tree that my grandpa and grandma on my mother's side started there is not one blood father in the family except my grandpa. They did have four girls and one boy. That could change of course but for now I find that very interesting. Same thing on my Dad's side. Their tree is smaller but I am the only blood father. Of course there is my Dad. Did you think of him initially? My wife and I were one of the first couples in our group of friends to have children as well. What I mean is I feel that there was a pretty big unknown when our first son Landis was born. I remember leaving the hospital with Landis and thinking, "wow they are really letting us leave with this little person". But hey you learn fast and love as much as you can. Every step along the way as a father has been mostly new but I embrace it and welcome the challenge. My wife and I talk about building traditions that our children will remember and hopefully cherish.

Mickey

I woke up on the day of my wedding very happy and excited for what was to come. I ate breakfast with some of the groomsman, shaved and we all got ready. We watched some TV (I don't remember what we watched) and waited for my wife and her bridesmaids to get ready. We took pictures before the wedding at different parks and areas around Downtown Seattle, which included people mooning us on Lake Union and some healthy advice to not get married. We got married on Seafair Sunday, which is always the first Sunday of August every year. It includes a hydroplane race on Lake Washington and an excuse to get drunk as well. There are lots of different events and things going on that weekend. We both grew up in the Seattle area and lived here our entire lives, oops guess we forgot about that one. I really do love Seattle but we are just not boat people. The irony of it all was we got married on a docked ferry boat. Anyway, we drove to the venue and waited for the ceremony to start. Throughout the day I wondered, what it would be like to have my dad at an event that was very special to me? Of course it was not the only thing I was thinking about. I did not realize even at the time, but now it means more to me that he was there and wanted to be there.

Three years after my brother got married and the get together at Denny's happened I somehow convinced my girlfriend of six years to marry me. During these three years I saw my dad off and on and it was really hard for me in the beginning. It was difficult to just start things up again. He had missed an incredible amount of time. I did the best I could to move forward though. We went to Mariners games or would go out to eat. I guess I was not really sure what we should do together.

As time went by I became more comfortable with seeing him, talking on the phone and in general being back in contact with him. It was just hard because there was not a lot of history there. As the time got closer to our wedding date, I knew I would need to make a decision.

Would we go to Australia or Hawaii for our honeymoon? It was a hard choice but we decided on Hawaii because we could get there much sooner and just be in the sun. Were you thinking of something else? Yes of course, would I invite my dad or not? Does he deserve to be there? Do I want him there? I put a lot of thought into this. It would be the first time that he would be at something important and special in my life. I, still to this day, am glad that I decided to invite him. My wife left it up to me and I believe I made the right choice, REMEMBER THAT. He was there in attendance with his fourth wife. He was not involved or in the wedding, but was there as a guest. I know he was happy that he was there. He has never told me that, but deep down I know. At least I think I know and that provides me with something that I had not had with my dad.

Our wedding colors were watermelon and no I did not pick them☺. I say this because about a week before the wedding I called my Dad. My decision to invite him had already long been made and he had let me know that he was coming. I asked if he would wear a solid lime green tie, remember I said solid lime green tie. What do you think when I say that? This was a request from my wife. We got married in Lake Union of Downtown Seattle. It was a beautiful August day and I feel great about everything that happened that day, except for a few things. I did not see my Dad initially because we were getting ready (which means a lot of waiting for everybody to get there) but I did hear about his tie choice. I did not believe it until I saw it! I really did not understand how my words could turn into that. I started to question myself, wait did I ask him to wear a giant bright colored Mickey Mouse tie? I was pretty positive I did not. Needless to say I was a little surprised. Needless to say my wife was not very happy about Mickey joining us at the wedding. Needless to say my brother, my dad, Mickey and I took some photos together; those pictures did not make our wedding book. Needless to say deep down I was disappointed, but also weirdly curious.

I laughed about it pretty quickly as time went by, but all of me wishes he would have just done what I had asked him to do. I know he did not purposely wear this tie to make things hard. Do you know how I know this? At one point while we were talking he points down to his tie and says look I wore a lime green tie! I believe he pointed this out because he really thought the tie was ok. Why else would he say that? At this point I started to question my eye sight! He was pointing to a very small part of the tie in the background of our friend Mickey. To this day I am still puzzled and confused about the tie. I guess some people's interpretation of what a solid lime green tie can be different. This is funny and I hope you are laughing but what it comes down to for me is he had another chance to come through. I have never really asked him for a lot and this time I did, that part is hard. I know it is just a stupid tie but it would have meant a lot more to me if he had just worn a watermelon green tie, but we would not have this story then, would we. When was the last time Mickey brought anything but fun and excitement? However, I still would have rather had my dad and Mickey than neither of them there. I can tell you this, whatever our kids want me to wear at their wedding, done! Another lesson learned I guess, right or wrong.

Another small note, we got married on a Sunday. We were in Hawaii on Monday enjoying the sun. I believe we had earned it!

Always There

I have always admired my Mom's hard work. She did a lot on her own and unfortunately I know this is all too common with single mothers. Why? Dads have just as much responsibility to be a parent as moms do. My Mom was there for every one of my basketball games in high school but one. My Dad was not there for even one. I probably played in about 90 to 100 games over the four years. My Mom was at every single graduation from preschool up to college. My Dad was at zero. I am pretty sure he knows that people graduate. I know my Mom worked hard to fill in the pieces that he did not fill, but no one can really do that. I know a lot of people say things like this, but I am not sure who or what I would be without my Mom.

She always believed in me, even when I struggled as a student in school or countless other times. I love my Mom! She was always there present and supporting. She is now doing that for our children as well. I know my Mom loves me unconditionally and it is hard to find people like this in life. How many people will support you no matter what? We should all strive to be people who do this. When I think about my Mom and Dad this is truly what it comes down to for me. My Mom was there, is there and will always be there. The greatest thing we can do as adults is be there for children to support them to be their best; whether that is a parent, uncle, aunt, grandma, grandpa, cousin or friend. Every child deserves this!

There is one story that really encompasses my mom. When I was young I used to go and play in these University of Washington

Basketball Camps in the summer. One year things came together and the team I was on won the camp for our age division. It was really cool and still remember being a part of it. I was probably around 11 or 12. I remember that it was fun and everyone on the team contributed and did their part. At the end of the camp they always had these award ceremonies, well I had never won anything the previous years that I had been a part of the camps. That is until this year! As they were announcing the different awards and we got closer to our division I did not really think about winning anything, but I did. I am not telling this story to brag (still have the trophy though). I really just want to let you know about my Mom's reaction when I did win the MVP of our division that year. It was animal like. She let out the biggest scream that could be heard across the entire campus. Was I embarrassed? No, I loved that she was there and proud of me.

Robert Landis

This is by far the hardest chapter for me to write in this book. I believe it is because he is the only person I am writing about who I can no longer talk too. I really had to think long and hard about what I wanted to say.

I run to get the newspaper, really the sports page. And yes people actually used to read the news on paper. "Grandpa will you read the sports section to me". I would go over and sit with him in a chair in the living room and we would read together, well I guess he would read and I would listen. It would turn out that I actually learned to read by reading about sports. My grandpa was there for his family, actually around and involved with his children and grandchildren. He was there for birthdays, holidays, graduations, etc. He was there and that is what I remember!

My grandpa on my mother's side was the only father that I knew in our family when I was growing up. He was the only father that was there and involved in his children's lives. Unfortunately his time came far too early. I was only seventeen when he passed away. He was also sick for a long time before that. He did not meet the great grandson's that carry his name or see me become a father. I still very much miss him even though it has been almost 20 years since he left us.

I really wish we could talk about how much I enjoy being a father, but also how hard it is at times. Honestly, I would love to hear from him how proud he is of me. At least I hope he would be proud of me. I believe my grandpa not only made an impact as a father with his own children but also with his grandchildren. That is what I hope to do moving forward. I want to have a positive impact!

He was actually a positive fatherly role model, what a concept. He cared about his children and wanted the best for them and you could feel that. I don't believe that you can fake this.

Landis asks about his great grandfather, probably because he knows where his name came from. I do wonder if it is more than that though. I think he knows that he was a special part of our family.

I love you grandpa and would love to stop by Albertsons to get some low calorie donuts with you! This is what he used to call donuts from one of local grocery stores, and no of course they were not low cal. Maybe I will actually do that today. That would be more than just a donut to me. I wonder, is it harder to lose people who we love or is it harder to accept that people that are still here lose us from not enough love?

Lovie Love

I have lived with two women, you know one and the other of course is my wife. We started dating late 2001 around Thanksgiving. I knew pretty quickly, probably within about a month, that something was very special about her. She pretended and played hard to get but she felt the same way. I think a lot of people thought we would not last very long when we started dating because we were so different then. Ha, in your face! As time has passed we have become more similar though. She has become a little quieter and I have become a little more talkative. My wife is very straight forward and honest (sometimes too much☺). She challenges and believes in me, another trait that she shares with my mom. Gina challenges me to think about things from a different perspective. She believes in me and supports me to do the things that I am capable of. Like completing my Master's Degree or becoming a college instructor. She has been supportive throughout with my Dad, even at times when it has been uncomfortable for her. She also calls my Dad "dickey", yes his name is Richard but to my knowledge he has never gone by Dick. Her own way of adding some humor to the situation I guess.

I look forward to the future with my wife and raising our children together. I know there will be times that will be hard and great times as well. I think we have already developed traditions for our kids and I can't wait to do these things every year with them. It makes me realize that I do not have one single tradition that I remember that involved my Dad. Those experiences are not there with my Dad. At times I believe we don't know how important a particular decision is, but going back (not an option). I wonder if my Dad thinks about this the way I do? Do I want to know?

I believe I really had to learn how to be a husband. I really don't want to sound like my wife trained me (she will love that I said that), but I did not have a role model for this. I really had no idea, which is no excuse. I work hard to be the best husband I can be and it is much harder after you have children. My experience of not having my Dad there left me with deep feelings and I knew what I did not want to do with my children, but being a husband was different. It requires a lot of giving and reflection. I struggle with being a person that does not ask people for things very often and I have worked on this with my wife. I have worked on communicating better and explaining what I actually mean. I think if I am always coming from a place where we are on the same team that is where we will end as well. I do think that being a good dad goes hand and hand with being a good husband. I know a lot of people say things like this, but I am not sure who or what I would be without my wife.

When I met Gina from the start I felt like she was that last piece of a puzzle that I had been looking at uncompleted. I could finally see what the puzzle looked like! And I am not telling you what the puzzle is. She is one of the few people who really knows me. I don't let everybody see the real me but with her it is easy. She allows me to be who I am. I don't need to pretend when I am around her and that is so refreshing. Gina and I have some of the most real conversations about life, family, friends and reality TV (most important) that I have ever had. She has helped me release the real me.

I do things for my wife that I would not do for anyone else, like watching fashion shows or wearing clothes that I highly dislike. She might say otherwise. Things are not always perfect and we are very busy. It takes a lot of hard work and effort to support each other. It also takes a lot of looking at yourself. I cannot wait until the kids get older and I can have reflective conversations with them. It will surely be a new experience for me, as just about everything with fatherhood has been. I hope we can help and support our children with their future decisions together. I already made the best decision I could in the fall of 2001.

Who Gives Who?

Our children give me so much and they don't even know it. I am very honored to be their father. The little things are what I care about and are important to me. I love to read them books every night before they go to bed, although sometimes I just want them to go to sleep. I love being there Christmas morning to see them excited and wondering what is in all those boxes.

Being a parent is not easy and I don't want to make it sound that way. IT IS VERY HARDWORK! It is beyond worth it though. It can have lasting affects across generations. What is more important than that? Still sometimes they do drive my wife and I crazy. Even in those times I love being there for them.

In the dictionary (and no I did not look in an actual dictionary). The definition of "dad" says, a person's father. However, the definition of "father" says, a man who gives care and protection to someone or something. Gives care and protection, I am pretty sure you need to be in close proximity to do those things. I would say that our kids are both a someone and a something, but I work hard every day to protect and care for them and not just be "a person's father". Anybody can do that! Anything that is worth having takes really hard work. I want to be there every day!

My wife and I are fortunate to have people in our lives that will give us a break so we can spend time together or with our friends. We feel very lucky and thankful for this. I believe this time supports us to be stronger and re-charged parents. Parenting is like going on a road trip with no map or these days no cell phone. Some days you find this awesome place and other days you end up in the ditch. Some days you feel like your car could fly or float and other days the most annoying song comes on over and over and over again. Some days endless arguing comes from the backseat and other days the absolute funniest things are said that you will remember forever. But, you always keep driving because tomorrow could be, well you know. Who does give to who? I hope that as a family we all give to each other.

Top Ten

What are the top ten days in your life? The days that define who you are or what you have done. The days that likely the most important people in your life are there and supporting. The days that I wish I could bottle and take a small sip on other days when I really need it. My wife and I have talked about these days and how special these days are. For most people and us included these days are getting married, the day our children were born, any other major accomplishment, graduation, the Seahawks winning the Super Bowl, any awesome vacation days, etc. These days are great and I wish my Dad would have been there to support me during these days, but I am currently 38 years old so I have lived somewhere around 13,870 days on this earth. The top ten days account for way less than 1% of my days. My Dad was not there for the top ten (except that the wedding of course), but honestly it would have been more important if he would have been around for the other 13,860! Because, if he was there for those you know he would have been there for those special days.

You would have to kill me to prevent me from being there for our children on these special days. You can say that for the other days as well. Top ten or not I will be there for our children to make every day the most that I can, because a day can provide every way possible to be a parent that cares.

Super dad vs. Everyday dad

There is no "super dad" in my humble opinion. No one is perfect! Every parent makes mistakes and it might be because you're tired, stressed, worried or hungry. Accept that and move on, however there is everyday dad. I hope I know this guy! This guy fixes toys over and over and over again. This guy watches the same movies over and over and over again. This guy reads the same books over and over and over again. This guy answers the same questions over and over and over again. This guy folds clothes or washes the same load of laundry over and over and over again. This guy cleans throw up out of his hair or poop from well you know. This guy listens to his kids but also has clear expectations. This guy wears costumes on Halloween that could be too tight or too short or really itchy, or it might not even be Halloween. This guy will eat whatever is left over from their kid's plates. This guy is everyday dad not super just there to do the super little things that need to get done. I try and be this dad every day, some days I do it some days I need to work harder but every day is a new opportunity.

When I was growing up my mom would travel for work and I would go and stay with some close family friends. The Sheehan's have their own children (three) but I always felt very comfortable and welcomed when I was there. Mike was actually my preschool teacher when I was just a little guy. Mike came to every graduation that I ever had. I believe that says a lot. He did not have to do that. We actually ended up working at the same place doing the same job for about a year and a half, and it was pretty cool. I could tell that he was proud. I would consider Mike an "everyday dad". He cares about his three children. Mike and his family are one of the few people that we also trust with our own children. I think that says a lot as well. What else can I say, Mike made a difference. Mike is also someone who I can talk with about my Dad and he will listen and I very much appreciate that.

Someday Is Here

A day would come at some point where the situation with my Dad would come up with our children. I knew they would ask questions. I just did not know when. I don't want to lie to them but I also want to be honest. When the kids see my Dad they do call him Grandpa Richard. Does Grandma Mary (my mother) have more meaning? Of course it does, but not sure how else to really deal with that one. He is still their grandpa. Our oldest son Landis had not asked about any of this. Almost to the day of his six birthday it came up, not with me but with my Mom.

Landis was with my Mom one morning (just the two of them). He started asking her questions about what happened with her and my Dad. I am not sure where these questions came from but my Mom started to explain to him the best she could what happened. Landis asked her why did my Grandpa Richard leave? How old was my dad when this happened? Did my dad still see Grandpa Richard after he left? I wish there were more positive answers to these questions but obviously by now you know there are not.

I love our children and will do whatever is humanly possible for them, but I am not going to lie to them. If they ask about my Dad I will tell them the story or I guess someday they will hopefully read this!

The conversation with Landis and my Mom ended by him saying something that I will never forget. It is what I work hard for every day. It is what I want most. It is what I did not have. Just one sentence by him. Whenever I think about it will fill up my emotional cup to the point of overflowing. My Mom was honest with Landis and had to tell him that Grandpa Richard was really not around when I was growing up.

If you only remember one thing from this book remember this sentence, remember how we should all be proud in making a difference in any child's life. I will work hard for the rest of my days to support our children to be the best they can be. I feel like we have only just begun and there is so much more to go but I look forward to it all. Anyway, sorry back to the sentence; with tears in his eyes Landis said, "Well so my Dad did not have the kind of dad I do". I have so many days (I hope about another 18,000 days or so) left to support them and be the dad that they deserve. All I can really say is: thank you Landis. Thank you, I cannot tell you how much that means to me.

A Lot's in a Name

My Mom and I are walking to the courthouse in Downtown Seattle, it is 1998 and I am 21 years old. Changing my last name is something that I have always thought about and today is the day. It is a sunny day and my Mom is going with me on her lunch break. Smith, the last name I was born with, but I must move on. Jeffers, however is my mother's family name and what I have always identified with. I grew up a Smith but will live on as a Jeffers. Man that is a little intense! Of course I am good with this and have thought a lot about doing this. I am proud but also sad. Proud to have the courage to do this. Sad because Aaron Smith is the only name I have ever known. I know my Dad will not appreciate this and for some reason I still care a little.

As we wait in the courtroom for the judge to call me and ask if I am changing my name because of debt, for criminal reasons or something else. I am torn as usual. I wish I did not need to do this, but I do feel I just have no choice. I am sure I am doing the right thing! The right thing I am not sure if that is even the way to say it.

On this day I have not seen my dad in 8 years and I will not see him for another 5 years. Today though I don't know that, I am not sure I will ever see him again! The judge calls my name and I go up and answer the question, it is over very fast. I am now a Jeffers, but I think I really have always been anyway. My grandfather on my mother's side who passed away four years ago was named Robert Jeffers and I am now Aaron Robert Jeffers. Our second son will be Gannon Robert Jeffers. I know Gannon Robert Smith would have felt a lot different.

My Mom, as usual was there that day to support me, but it would have been weird for me if she did not. That kind of trust and guidance can only come from time and care, lots and lots of care.

It takes me a long time to get used to the name but it definitely suits me. Today 17 years later I don't even think about it really. Most of our friends know me as Jeffers and that is just fine with me.

Smith of course was my Dad's last name, which is a very common last name. Smith which I received from my Dad but he did not earn. Jeffers, which our kids carry and I hope I will earn.

My wife's maiden name was Piampanichwat, try and pronounce it I dare you. Side note one day we were in Walgreens my wife was not feeling well and the pharmacist said on the loud speaker would Regina P ....., would Regina come to the back counter. She did not even try to pronounce it! Okay I won't leave you guessing how to pronounce it: p-m-pan-ich-a-wat. Anyway, because her name was so hard to pronounce she used to tell people her name was .... Smith. I guess we both ended up leaving that name behind. There really is a lot in a name, at least for me there is.

Forgive but Remember

I do believe in my heart that I have been able to forgive my Dad for all of the time lost and hurt. I will never forget what happened though. It is a part of me and always will be, and at times I want to remember because I don't want to repeat things that occurred to me. I look at it this way, we all have things that happen in our lives and we can either choose to learn from them or not. It took me a long time to get to this point and it only happened when I was ready to do it. Forgiving him gave me a better path to being a better and happier person. I forgave him for myself! I think if I did it for anyone else it just would not have worked.

I used to wish what happened when I was growing up did not happen or people would change, but people are who they are and do what they do. I used to wish that my Dad lived in another state or was in jail. I wanted there to be reason why he was not there. There was no reason though. I have forgiven him, but he missed out. Everyone makes mistakes all the time, but what my Dad did was an ongoing really messed up mistake. He got up every morning and had the opportunity to make a different decision. I have worked hard on moving past that, not easy! I feel I have always had challenges with having people in my corner who want to be there. I really try and live in the present but it is something I work hard at every day. I look at life a lot differently now than I used to, but I assume that everyone does. I wish I could talk to myself at 10 years old or 15 or 25. Wait, I guess my Dad should have been there to do that. If I was able to talk to myself when I was 10 I would say that it was not my fault that I did nothing to cause all of this. I would tell the 10 year old me to not worry about it as much and try and be 10. I would tell the 15 year old me to keep playing basketball and really give it your all, also to study harder and open up to friends more. I would tell the 25 year old me that you will see your dad soon and eventually it will improve. It will never be how we want it to be, but it will be better. I will also tell the 25 year old me that you will be a dad and your kids will be awesome! You will love being a father and in 2015 there will be a new STAR WARS movie and your kids will love it. I wonder what the 57 year old me would tell me now? I can tell you what I hope he would say: that your kids are still awesome and doing their best at whatever they are doing. I hope he would say that I had a close and great relationship with them and I really knew them. Crazy to even think, but in 20 years they will of course be adults. Landis would be about the age that I started to see my Dad again. I cannot imagine missing those years.

Future > Past

Since 2007 the relationship has improved with my Dad. I see him mostly with my family three or four times a year. I think we would likely see him more if he did not live in Tacoma, WA which is about an hour and a half away from where we live in Lynnwood, WA. He will bring stuff for our children and get dinner when he comes with his wife. I have become more at peace with where things are now with my Dad. It took a very long time to arrive at this place and I am glad that I was able to reach this point. For a long time I thought how things are now would never be possible. I don't get nervous to see him anymore, which in itself is a really big step. Do I want more? I hate having to think about that question. There is no doubt in my mind that I made this choice for myself. Why can't I see my Dad now? I came to the conclusion that there was no reason why not, really the only reason was being able to forgive what happened.

I am not 100 percent sure what is next for my Dad and I, but I do know what is in the rearview mirror and I am doing my best to not look back but look forward. I do know that things are different now than when I was growing up. I definitely don't think about it as much as I used to. When I was younger I used to think about it a lot. At times I let it control me. That is no one's fault but mine! At times I felt I was in a fog. Was I doing my best? Something was holding me back. It was frustrating, but I was doing it to myself and I own that. I was a terrible student in high school, but the longer I went to school the better I did. I feel that way with my career as well. I work in the Early Childhood Field following in my Mom's footsteps. I do wish I could have found my way out of the fog earlier, but live and learn I guess. I want our children to never enter this fog. I want them to do their best at everything they put their mind to. I am not perfect and I am still working on all of this, but I have worked very hard and I am proud of that.

My son has told me more than a few times, "Dad I want to be a teacher like you were". I have no idea if he will be a teacher or not. I just want him to be happy. I hope he is saying this because he wants to be like his father. I hope that I continue to be the type of person he wants to be like and a positive role model. I am sorry to say this, but again back to decisions. I never said I want to be a firefighter. I wonder why that is? I respect and appreciate what firefighters do, everyone does but for me it was much more than that. I do remember wanting to be like my mom though. By the way my mom was and is a preschool teacher, childcare director, childcare administrator, college instructor and grandma extraordinaire.

I Will ...

I will. That means you can count on it happening. It means one would do everything possible to follow through and do what they said they would do. It is very important to me that our children know that when I say, "I will" that outside of Sasquatch himself kidnapping me that it will happen. I will be there at graduations. I will support them unconditionally with what they want to do (within reason). I will be a positive role model to the best of my abilities every day. I will never put our boys in a position where they feel like a choice has to be made to see me or not. I will show them how to shave. I will teach them how to ride a bike. I will do homework with them. I will read to them. I will not let them wear Yankees, 49ers, Patriots or University of Oregon gear. I will teach them about sports. I will encourage their best. I will believe them. I will be there during the great times and the not so great times. I will do my best to pick them up when they are down. I will laugh with them. I will cook for them and with them. I will take care of myself. I will create another generation of Seattle Sports Fans. I will have memories that I will never forget. I will tell them stories about how I saw Ken Griffey Jr., Edgar Martinez and Randy Johnson play. I will explain how awesome Gary Payton and Shawn Kemp were together (god I miss the Sonics). I will tell them about the Kingdome, the 1991 Washington Huskies football team that won the National Championship, 1995 Double by Edgar that probably saved baseball in Seattle and 43 to 8 over Denver and heartbreak the next year against New England. I will not be perfect and I will make mistakes. I know that too. I will encourage them to live in the moment. I will go to a galaxy far, far away with them. I know there are so many things that I am not even thinking of and that I will want to do for them. Check back in a year or five or ten. I will still be here being the best father I can be. Will I? Well, I love our children and I am boldly determined. Love and determination, I am honored to accept the ride on the roller coaster, lets buckle that seat belt and go! We should all be so lucky to have the opportunity to make a difference.

I will leave you with this quote from the great philosopher "Gannon" he said, "Dad don't be shell fish". I really love how honest children can be, but I would not have this memory if I was not there every day with our boys. I don't deserve any kind of medal or recognition for this, because it is what every mother or father should be doing. How different would the world be if both parents supported every child in a positive way? Experiences and decisions that is what I believe being a parent is all about. Gannon, I will try everyday not to be shell fish. You have my word and promise! I don't even like seafood anyway!

Game On

They reach half court and the pass goes to the wing, he raises up to take the shot! They need a three to tie the game, and the shot goes in. They are calling it a two, so right now the game is over and they will have to just be happy and fortunate with the two. As the refs go to the monitor to check to see if the shot was taken from behind the three point line, this will determine if the game continues. The process of identifying the shot as a two or three is taking much longer than anyone could have ever imagined.

We have been waiting for five years to see if the game will continue. Wait, the refs are coming together and yes the shot is a three! Boy oh boy, no we have two of those already this time it is girl power. What will the rest of the game look like now after all of this time? You know when you are watching an incredibly well played and entertaining game you always want more. You want the game to continue on because the game is so fun to watch, well I hope we will continue to make this game a classic!

A girl, A GIRL! Wow I cannot believe what an amazing turn of events. I know our boys will love her. I know we will love her. I will need to learn a lot of new stuff, but I will put everything I can into it. Alright, let's continue on in this game. I look forward to another adventure in our family that I know will bring many wonderful memories. In the coming years I hope to have so many powerful, funny and amazing things to share about our ever growing family.

Seriously, this is it though. I am not kidding! Two + One = we have so much love already.

After All

I wish I could say at one point my Dad and I had this deep and bonding conversation, but we never have. I don't think we ever will, but you never know. I am happy when I see him now, which is oddly enough for me. Things may never be how I had hoped they would be when I was young, however they are better than I thought they would be 10 years ago. I did not choose my Dad, but I choose to see him now. I think he knows that he will likely always be on thin ice, but hey I get the feeling that he actually thinks about me at times. My Dad did tell me awhile back that he loved me! Crazy, right! First time I had ever heard that from him, just a little late but better late than never. I do hope at some point maybe we can have that catch that we never had when I was growing up. All it takes is two gloves and a ball, fathers and sons do that all the time right. Well, that is not something that I am used to. But you know what, our children sure will! Landis, Gannon and Nyah grab your gloves lets go outside and play catch. We could wait but waiting is always dangerous and you never know what you will miss out on.

55515027R00033

Made in the USA
San Bernardino, CA
02 November 2017